I CAN
DO IT®

ALSO BY

LOUISE HAY

BOOKS

FOR CHILDREN

The Adventures of Lulu
I Think, I Am! (with Kristina Tracy)
Lulu and the Ant: A Message of Love
Lulu and the Dark: Conquering Fears
Lulu and Willy the Duck: Learning Mirror Work

AUDIO PROGRAMS

All Is Well (audio book)
Anger Releasing
Cancer
Change and Transition
Dissolving Barriers
Embracing Change
The Empowering Women Gift Collection
Feeling Fine Affirmations
Forgiveness/Loving the Inner Child
How to Love Yourself
Meditations for Loving Yourself to Great Health
(with Ahlea Khadro and Heather Dane)
Meditations for Personal Healing
Meditations to Heal Your Life (audio book)
Morning and Evening Meditations
101 Power Thoughts
Overcoming Fears
The Power Is Within You (audio book)
The Power of Your Spoken Word
Receiving Prosperity
Self-Esteem Affirmations (subliminal)
Self-Healing
Stress-Free (subliminal)
Totality of Possibilities
What I Believe and Deep Relaxation
You Can Heal Your Life (audio book)

You Can Heal Your Life Study Course
Your Thoughts Create Your Life

DVDS

Receiving Prosperity
You Can Heal Your Life Study Course
You Can Heal Your Life, THE MOVIE
(also available in an expanded edition)
You Can Trust Your Life (with Cheryl Richardson)

CARD DECKS

Heart Thoughts Cards
How to Love Yourself Cards
I Can Do It® Cards
Life Loves You Cards (with Robert Holden)
Power Thought Cards

CALENDAR

I Can Do It® Calendar (for each individual year)

THE ESSENTIAL LOUISE HAY COLLECTION

(comprising *You Can Heal Your Life*, *Heal Your Body*,
and *The Power Is Within You* in a single volume)

All of the above are available at your local bookstore,
or may be ordered by visiting:

Hay House USA: www.hayhouse.com®
Hay House Australia: www.hayhouse.com.au
Hay House UK: www.hayhouse.co.uk
Hay House India: www.hayhouse.co.in

LOUISE HAY

I CAN DO IT®

- -

HOW TO USE AFFIRMATIONS TO CHANGE YOUR LIFE

HAY HOUSE, INC.

Carlsbad, California • New York City

London • Sydney • New Delhi

Published in the United States by: Hay House, Inc.: www.hayhouse.com®
Published in Australia by: Hay House Australia Pty. Ltd.: www.hayhouse
.com.au • Published in the United Kingdom by: Hay House UK, Ltd.:
www.hayhouse.co.uk • Published in India by: Hay House Publishers India:
www.hayhouse.co.in

COVER AND INTERIOR DESIGN: Karla Baker
INTERIOR ILLUSTRATIONS: *Watercolor Winter Florals* © Erika Firm and
Circle Vector Patterns © Gudiny via Creative Market

**Library of Congress Cataloging-in-Publication Data
for the Original Edition**

Hay, Louise L.
I can do it! : how to use affirmations to change your life / Louise L. Hay.
p. cm.
ISBN 1-4019-0219-7
    1. Affirmations. 2. Self-talk. 3. Change (Psychology) I. Title.
    BF697.5.S47H388 2004
    158—dc21   2003003792

Tradepaper ISBN: 978-1-4019-6560-0
E-book ISBN: 978-1-4019-1961-0
Audiobook ISBN: 978-1-4019-6664-5

10 9 8 7 6 5 4 3
1st edition, January 2004
2nd edition, August 2021

Printed in the United States of America

I DEDICATE THIS LITTLE BOOK
TO MY EVER-GROWING
AUDIENCE.
IT IS MY DESIRE
THAT EACH AND EVERY
PERSON LEARN HOW TO
USE AFFIRMATIONS
TO CREATE LOVE, PEACE,
JOY, PROSPERITY,
AND A SENSE OF
WELL-BEING
FOR THEMSELVES.

CONTENTS

BONUS CONTENT

Thank you for purchasing *I Can Do It* by Louise Hay. This product includes a free download of the full audiobook! To access this bonus content, please visit www.hayhouse.com/download and enter the Product ID and Download Code as they appear below.

Product ID: 856

Download Code: ebook

For further assistance, please contact Hay House Customer Care by phone: US (800) 654-5126 or INTL CC+(760) 431-7695 or visit www.hayhouse.com/contact.

Thank you again for your Hay House purchase. Enjoy!

In conjunction with (or after) reading the book, listen to the audio download for at least 30 days. If you drive a car, this audio is a perfect companion while you're on the road. Let these ideas permeate your consciousness until they become a part of you.

PUBLISHER'S NOTE

Hay House products are intended to be powerful, inspirational, and life-changing tools for personal growth and healing. They are not intended as a substitute for medical care. Please use this audio program under the supervision of your care provider. Neither the author nor Hay House, Inc., assumes any responsibility for your improper use of this product.

THE POWER OF AFFIRMATIONS

Today is a new day. Today is a day for you to begin creating a joyous, fulfilling life. Today is the day to begin to release all your limitations. Today is the day for you to learn the secrets of life. You can change your life for the better. You already have the tools within you to do so. These tools are your thoughts and your beliefs. In this book, I will teach you how to use these tools to improve the quality of your life.

For those of you who aren't familiar with the benefits of positive affirmations, I'd like to explain a little about them. An affirmation is really anything you say or think. A lot of what we normally say and think is quite negative and doesn't create good experiences for us. We have to retrain our thinking and speaking into positive patterns if we want to change our lives. An affirmation opens the door. It's a beginning point on the path to change. In essence, you're saying to your subconscious mind: *"I am taking responsibility. I am aware that there is something I can do to change."* When I talk about *doing affirmations*, I mean consciously choosing words that will either help *eliminate* something from your life or help *create* something new in your life. Every thought you think and every word you speak is an affirmation.

All of our self-talk, our internal dialogue, is a stream of affirmations. You're using affirmations every moment whether you know it or not. You're affirming and creating your life experiences with every word and thought. Your beliefs are merely habitual thinking patterns that you learned as a child. Many of them work very well for you. Other beliefs may be limiting your ability to create the very things you say you want. What you want and what you believe you deserve may be very different. You need to pay attention to your thoughts so that you can begin to eliminate the ones creating experiences you do *not* want in your life.

Please realize that every complaint is an affirmation of something you think you don't want in your life. Every time you get angry, you're affirming that you want more anger in your life. Every time you feel like a victim, you're affirming that you want to *continue* to feel like a victim. If you feel that Life isn't giving you what you want in your world, then it's certain that you will never have the goodies that Life gives to others—that is, until you change the way you think and talk.

You're not a bad person for thinking the way you do. You've just never learned *how* to think and talk. People throughout the world are just now beginning to learn that our thoughts create our experiences. Your parents probably didn't know this, so they couldn't possibly teach it to you. They taught you how to look at life in the way that *their* parents taught them. So nobody is wrong. However, it's time for all of us to wake up and begin to consciously create our lives in a way that pleases and supports us. *You* can do it. *I* can do it. *We all* can do it—we just need to learn how. So let's get to it. Throughout this book, I'll talk about affirmations in general, and then I'll get to specific areas of life and show you how to make positive changes in your health, your finances, your love life, and so on. This is a small book, because once you learn how to use affirmations, then you can apply the principles in all situations.

Some people say that "affirmations don't work" (which is an affirmation in itself), when what they mean is that they don't know how to use them correctly. They may say, *"My prosperity is growing,"* but then think, *Oh, this is stupid, I know it won't work.* Which affirmation do you think will win out? The negative one, of course, because it's part of a long-standing, habitual way of looking at life. Sometimes people will say their affirmations once a day and complain the rest of the time. It will take a long time for affirmations to work if they're done that way. The complaining affirmations will always win, because there are more of them and they're usually said with great feeling.

However, *saying* affirmations is only part of the process. What you do the rest of the day and night is even more important. The secret to having your affirmations work quickly and consistently is to prepare an atmosphere for them to grow in. Affirmations are like seeds planted in soil. Poor soil, poor growth. Rich soil, abundant growth. The more you choose to think thoughts that make you feel good, the quicker the affirmations work. So think happy thoughts, it's that simple. And it *is* doable. The way you choose to think, right now, is just that—a choice. You may not realize it because you've thought this way for so long, but it really is a choice. Now . . . today . . . this moment . . . you can choose to change your thinking. Your life won't turn around overnight, but if you're consistent and make the choice on a daily basis to think thoughts that make you feel good, you'll definitely make positive changes in every area of your life.

(I learned this secret from Esther Hicks/Abraham. Esther Hicks is a motivational speaker who dialogues with a group of spiritual teachers who call themselves Abraham. If you haven't experienced the teacher Abraham, visit www.Abraham-Hicks.com for more information. I consider Abraham to be one of the best teachers on the planet today.)

I wake up each morning with blessings and gratitude for the wonderful life I lead, and I make the choice to think happy thoughts no matter what others are doing. No, I don't do this 100 percent of the time, but I am up to about 75 or 80 percent right now, and it's made a big difference in how much I enjoy life and how much good just seems to flow into my everyday world.

The only moment you ever live in is *this* moment. It's the only time you have any control over. "Yesterday is history, tomorrow is a mystery, today is a gift, which is why we call it the *present*." My yoga teacher, Maureen MacGinnis, repeats this in every class she teaches. If you don't choose to feel good in this moment, then how can you create future moments that are abundant and fun?

How do you feel right now? Do you feel good? Do you feel bad? What are your current emotions? What is your gut feeling? Would you like to feel better? Then reach for a better feeling or thought. If you feel bad in any way—sad, grumpy, bitter, resentful, angry, fearful, guilty, depressed, jealous, critical, and so on—then you've temporarily lost your connection to the flow of good experiences that the Universe has waiting for you. Don't waste your thoughts on blame. No person, place, or thing has any control over your feelings because they don't think in your mind.

This is also why you really have no control over others—you see, you can't control their thoughts. No one can control another unless that person gives permission. So you want to be aware of this powerful mind you have. You can take total control over your own thinking. It's the only thing you'll ever have total control of. What you choose to think is what you'll get in life. I've chosen to think thoughts of joy and appreciation, and you can, too.

What kinds of thoughts make *you* feel good? Thoughts of love, appreciation, gratitude, joyful childhood experiences? Thoughts in which you rejoice that you're alive and bless your body with love? Do you truly enjoy this present moment and get excited about to-morrow? Thinking these kinds of thoughts is an act of loving yourself, and loving yourself creates miracles in your life.

Now let's get to the affirmations. Doing affirmations is consciously choosing to think certain thoughts that will create positive results in the future. They create a focal point that will allow you to begin changing your thinking. Affirmative statements are *going beyond the reality of the present into the creation of the future through the words you use in the now.*

When you choose to say *"I am very prosperous,"* you may actually have very little money in the bank at the moment, but what you're doing is planting seeds for future prosperity. Each time you repeat this statement, you're reaffirming the seeds you've planted in the atmosphere of your mind. That's why you want it to be a *happy* atmosphere. Things grow more quickly in fertile, rich soil.

It's important for you to always say your affirmations in the *present* tense, and without contractions. (Although I use contractions throughout the running text of my books, I never use them in affirmations, since I don't want to diminish their power.) For example, typical affirmations would start: *"I have . . ."* or *"I am . . ."* If you say, "I am going to . . ." or "I will have . . . ," then your thought stays out there in the future. The Universe takes your thoughts and words very literally and gives you what you say you want. *Always.* This is another reason to maintain a happy mental atmosphere. It's easier to think in positive affirmations when you feel good.

Think of it this way: Every thought you think counts, so don't waste your precious thoughts. Every positive thought brings good into your life. Every negative thought pushes good away; it keeps it just out of your reach. How many times in your life have you almost gotten something good and it seemed to be snatched away at the last moment? If you could remember what your mental atmosphere was like at those times, you'd have the answer. Too many negative thoughts create a barrier against positive affirmations.

If you say, "I don't want to be sick anymore," this is not an affirmation for good health. You have to state clearly what you *do* want. *"I accept perfect health now."*

"I hate this car" does not bring you a wonderful new car because you're not being clear. Even if you do get a new car, in a short time you'll probably hate it, because that's what you've been affirming. If you want a new car, then say something like this: *"I have a beautiful new car that suits all of my needs."*

You'll hear some people saying, "Life sucks!" (which is a terrible affirmation). Can you imagine what experiences *that* statement will attract to you? Of course, it isn't Life that sucks, it's your *thinking* that sucks. That thought will help you feel terrible. And when you feel terrible, no good can come into your life.

Don't waste time arguing for your limitations: poor relationships, problems, illnesses, poverty, and so on. The more you talk about the problem, the more you anchor it in place. Don't blame others for what's seemingly wrong in your life—that's just another waste of time. Remember, you're under the laws of your own consciousness, your own thoughts, and you attract specific experiences to you as a result of the way you think.

When you change your thinking process, then everything in your life will also change. You'll be amazed and delighted to see how people, places, things, and circumstances can change. Blame is just another negative affirmation, and you don't want to waste your precious thoughts on it. Instead, learn to turn your negative affirmations into positive ones. For instance:

I hate my body.	**BECOMES**	I love and appreciate my body.
I never have enough money.	**BECOMES**	Money flows into my life in an abundant way.
I'm tired of being sick.	**BECOMES**	I allow my body to return to its natural, vibrant health.
I'm too fat.	**BECOMES**	I honor my body and take good care of it.
Nobody loves me.	**BECOMES**	I radiate love, and love fills my life.
I'm not creative.	**BECOMES**	I am discovering talents I did not know I had.
I'm stuck in a lousy job.	**BECOMES**	Wonderful new doors are opening for me all the time.
I'm not good enough.	**BECOMES**	I am in the process of positive change, and I deserve the best.

This doesn't mean that you have to be worried about every thought you think. When you first begin to make the changeover and really pay attention to your thoughts, you'll be horrified to realize how negative much of your thinking has been. So when you catch a negative thought, just think to yourself, *That is an old thought; I no longer choose to think that way.* Then find a positive thought to replace it as quickly as you can. Remember, you want to feel good as much as possible. Thoughts of bitterness, resentment, blame, and guilt make you feel miserable. And that's a habit you really want to release.

Another barrier to allowing positive affirmations to work is feeling "not good enough"—that is, you feel that you don't deserve to have good in your life. If that's your issue, then you could begin with Chapter 8 (Self-Esteem). You could see how many of the self-esteem affirmations you can memorize, and then repeat them often. Doing so will help change that "worthless" feeling you might be carrying around, to one of self-worth. Then watch your positive affirmations materialize.

Affirmations are solutions that will replace whatever problem you might have. Whenever you have a problem, repeat over and over:

"All is well. Everything is working out for my highest good.

Out of this situation only good will come. I am safe."

This simple affirmation will work miracles in your life.

♥

I would also suggest that you avoid sharing your affirmations with others who may pooh-pooh these ideas. When you're just getting started, it's best to keep your thinking to yourself until you've achieved your desired results. Then your friends will say, "Your life is changing so much. You're so different. What have you been doing?"

Go over this Introduction several times until you really understand the principles and can live them. Also, zero in on the chapters that have the most meaning to you, and practice those particular affirmations. And remember to make up affirmations of your own.

Some affirmations you can use right now are:

"I can feel good about myself!"

"I can make positive changes in my life!"

"I can do it!"

CHAPTER 1

HEALTH

- - - - - - - - -

I am grateful for
my healthy body.
I love life.

If you want to create better health in your body, there are definitely some things you must *not* do: You must not get angry at your body for any reason. Anger is another affirmation, and it's telling your body that you hate it, or parts of it. Your cells are very aware of every thought you have. Think of your body as a servant that's working as hard as it can to keep you in perfect health no matter how you treat it.

Your body knows how to heal itself. If you feed it healthy foods and beverages, give it exercise and sufficient sleep, and think happy thoughts, then its work is easy. The cells are working in a happy, healthy atmosphere. However, if you're a couch potato who feeds your body junk food and lots of diet soda, and you skimp on sleep and are grouchy and irritable all the time, then the cells in your body are working at a disadvantage—they're in a disagreeable atmosphere. If this is the case, it's no wonder that your body isn't as healthy as you'd like it to be.

You'll never create good health by talking or thinking about your illness. Good health comes from love and appreciation. You want to put as much love into your body as you possibly can. Talk to it and stroke it in loving ways. If there's a part of your body that's ailing or dis-eased, then you want to treat it as you would a sick little child. Tell it how much you love it, and that you're doing everything you can to help it get well quickly.

If you're sick, then you want to do more than just go to the doctor and have him or her give you a chemical to take care of the symptom. Your body is telling you that something you're doing isn't good for your body. You need to learn more about health—the more you learn, the easier it is to take care of your body. You don't want to choose to feel like a victim. If you do, you'll just be giving your power away. You could go to a health-food store and pick up one of the many good books that teach you how to keep yourself healthy, or you could see a nutritionist and have a healthy diet created just for you, but whatever you do, create a healthy, happy mental atmosphere. Be a willing participant in your own health plan.

I believe that we create every so-called illness in our body. The body, like everything else in life, is a mirror of our inner thoughts and beliefs. Our body is always talking to us; we just need to take the time to listen. Every cell within our body responds to every single thought we think and every word we speak.

Continuous modes of thinking and speaking produce body behaviors and postures and "eases," or dis-eases. The person who has a permanently scowling face didn't produce that by having joyous, loving thoughts. Older people's faces and bodies so clearly show a lifetime of thinking patterns. How will you look when you're elderly?

Learn to accept that your life is not a series of random events, but a pathway of awakening. If you live every day in this way, you'll never grow old. You'll just keep growing. Imagine the day you turn 49 as the infancy of another life. A woman who reaches age 50 today and remains free of cancer and heart disease can expect to see her 92nd birthday. You and only you have the ability to customize your own life cycle. So change your thinking now and get going!

♥

You're here for a very important reason, and everything you need is available to you.

You can choose to think thoughts that create a mental atmosphere that contributes to illness, or you can choose to think thoughts that create a healthy atmosphere both within you and around you. (My book *Heal Your Body* is a comprehensive guide to the metaphysical causes of dis-ease, and it includes all the affirmations you'll need to overcome any ailment.)

POSITIVE
AFFIRMATIONS
FOR
HEALTH

I enjoy the foods that
are best for my body.
I love every cell of my body.

· • ● ◦ ·

I look forward to a healthy old
age because I take loving care
of my body now.

· • ● ◦ ·

I am constantly discovering new
ways to improve my health.

· • ● ◦ ·

I return my body to optimal health
by giving it what it needs on
every level.

· · ● ○ ·

I am pain free and totally
in sync with life.

· · ● ○ ·

Healing happens! I get my mind
out of the way and allow the
intelligence of my body to do its
healing work naturally.

· · ● ○ ·

My body is always doing its best
to create perfect health.

· · ● ○ ·

I balance my life between
work, rest, and play.
They all get equal time.

. •●• .

I am grateful to be alive today.
It is my joy and pleasure to live
another wonderful day.

. •●• .

I am willing to ask for
help when I need it. I always
choose the health professional
who is just right for my needs.

. •●• .

I trust my intuition. I am willing
to listen to that still, small
voice within.

· ·●· ·

I get plenty of sleep every night.
My body appreciates how
I take care of it.

· ·●· ·

I make healthy choices.
I have respect for myself.

· ·●· ·

I lovingly do everything I can to
assist my body in maintaining
perfect health.

· ·●· ·

I have a special guardian angel.
I am Divinely guided and
protected at all times.

·•◉•·

Perfect health is my Divine right,
and I claim it now.

·•◉•·

I devote a portion of my time to
helping others. It is good for my
own health.

·•◉•·

MORE
POSITIVE
AFFIRMATIONS
FOR
HEALTH

I am grateful for my healthy body.
I love life.

. • ● • ·

I am the only person who has
control over my eating habits.
I can always resist something
if I choose to.

. • ● • ·

Water is my favorite beverage.
I drink lots of water to cleanse
my body and mind.

. • ● • ·

Filling my mind with
pleasant thoughts is the
quickest road to health.

. . ● ○ .

My happy thoughts help
create my healthy body.

. . ● ○ .

I go within and connect
with that part of myself that
knows how to heal.

. . ● ○ .

I breathe deeply and fully.
I take in the breath of life,
and I am nourished.

. . ● ○ .

CHAPTER 2

FORGIVENESS

I am forgiving, loving,
gentle, and kind, and I know
that Life loves me.

You can never be free of bitterness as long as you continue to think unforgiving thoughts. How can you be happy in this moment if you continue to choose to be angry and resentful? Thoughts of bitterness can't create joy. No matter how justified you feel you are, no matter what "they" did, if you insist on holding on to the past, then you will never be free. Forgiving yourself and others will release you from the prison of the past.

When you feel that you're stuck in some situation, or when your affirmations aren't working, it usually means that there's more forgiveness work to be done. When you don't flow freely with life in the present moment, it usually means that you're holding on to a past moment. It can be regret, sadness, hurt, fear, guilt, blame, anger, resentment, or sometimes even a desire for revenge. Each one of these states comes from a space of unforgiveness, a refusal to let go and come in to the present moment. Only in the present moment can you create your future.

If you're holding on to the past, you can't be in the present. It's only in this "now" moment that your thoughts and words are powerful. So you really don't want to waste your current thoughts by continuing to create your future from the garbage of the past.

When you blame another, you give your own power away because you're placing the responsibility for your feelings on someone else. People in your life may behave in ways that trigger uncomfortable responses in you. However, they didn't get into your mind and create the buttons that have been pushed. Taking responsibility for your own feelings and reactions is mastering your "ability to respond." In other words, you learn to consciously choose rather than simply react.

Forgiveness is a tricky and confusing concept for many people, but know that there's a difference between forgiveness and acceptance. Forgiving someone doesn't mean that you condone their behavior! The act of forgiveness takes place in your own mind. It really has nothing to do with the other person. The reality of true forgiveness lies in setting yourself free from the pain. It's simply an act of releasing yourself from the negative energy that you've chosen to hold on to.

Also, forgiveness doesn't mean allowing the painful behaviors or actions of another to continue in your life. Sometimes forgiveness means letting go: You forgive that person and then you release them. Taking a stand and setting healthy boundaries is often the most loving thing you can do—not only for yourself, but for the other person as well.

No matter what your reasons are for having bitter, unforgiving feelings, you can go beyond them. You have a choice. You can choose to stay stuck and resentful, or you can do yourself a favor by willingly forgiving what happened in the past; letting it go; and then moving on to create a joyous, fulfilling life. You have the freedom to make your life anything you want it to be because you have freedom of *choice*.

POSITIVE
AFFIRMATIONS
FOR
FORGIVENESS

The door to my heart opens
inward. I move through
forgiveness to love.

· •●● ·

Today I listen to my feelings, and I
am gentle with myself. I know that
all of my feelings are my friends.

· •●● ·

The past is over, so it has no
power now.
The thoughts of this moment
create my future.

· •●● ·

It is no fun being a victim.
I refuse to be helpless anymore.
I claim my own power.

· •◉◦ ·

I give myself the gift of
freedom from the past, and
move with joy into the now.

· •◉◦ ·

I get the help I need when
I need it, from various sources.
My support system is
strong and loving.

· •◉◦ ·

There is no problem so big or
small that it cannot be solved
with love.

· •◉◦ ·

I am ready to be healed. I am
willing to forgive. All is well.

· ·●° ·

When I make a mistake,
I realize that it is only part of the
learning process.

· ·●° ·

I move beyond forgiveness
to understanding, and I have
compassion for all.

· ·●° ·

Each day is a new opportunity.
Yesterday is over and done. Today
is the first day of my future.

· ·●° ·

As I change my thoughts, the
world around me changes.

· ·●° ·

I know that old, negative
patterns no longer limit me.
I let them go with ease.

. . ● ○ .

I am forgiving, loving, gentle,
and kind, and I know that
Life loves me.

. . ● ○ .

As I forgive myself, it becomes
easier to forgive others.

. . ● ○ .

I love and accept my family
members exactly as they are
right now.

. . ● ○ .

MORE
POSITIVE
AFFIRMATIONS
FOR
FORGIVENESS

I forgive myself for not being perfect. I am living the very best way I know how.

' • ◉ ○ '

I cannot change another person. I let others be who they are, and I simply love who I am.

' • ◉ ○ '

It is now safe for me to release all of my childhood traumas and move into love.

' • ◉ ○ '

I know that I cannot take
responsibility for other people.
We are all under the law of
our own consciousness.

• • ● • •

I return to the basics of life:
forgiveness, courage, gratitude,
love and humor.

• • ● • •

Everyone in my life has
something to teach me. We have
a purpose in being together.

• • ● • •

I forgive everyone in my past
for all perceived wrongs.
I release them with love.

• • ● • •

All of the changes in life that
lie before me are positive ones.
I am safe.

CHAPTER 3

PROSPERITY

Life supplies all my needs
in great abundance.
I trust Life.

You can never create prosperity by talking
or thinking about your lack of money. This
is wasted thinking and cannot bring you
abundance. Dwelling on lack only creates more
lack. Poverty thinking brings more poverty.
Gratitude thinking brings abundance.

There are a few negative affirmations and attitudes that are guaranteed to keep prosperity beyond your reach—for example: *"I never have enough money!"* That's a terrible affirmation to use. Another unproductive one is: *"Money goes out faster than it comes in."* This is poverty thinking of the worst kind. The Universe can only respond to what you believe about yourself and your life. Examine whatever negative thoughts you have about money, and then decide to release them and let them go. They haven't served you well in the past and will not serve you well in the future.

Sometimes people think that their financial problems will be solved by inheriting money from a long-lost relative or winning the lottery. Sure, you can fantasize about such things, or even buy an occasional lottery ticket for fun, but please don't put a lot of attention on acquiring money in this way. This is *scarcity thinking,* or *poverty thinking,* and it won't bring lasting good into your life. Anyway, when it comes to the lottery, winning seldom brings positive changes into anyone's life. In fact, within two years, most lottery winners have lost almost all of their money, have nothing to show for it, and are often worse off financially than before. The problem with money acquired in this way is that it rarely solves any problems. Why? Because it doesn't involve changing your consciousness. In effect, you're saying to the Universe: "I don't deserve to have good in my life except by a fluke chance."

♥

If you would only change your consciousness, your thinking, to allow the abundance of the Universe to flow through your experience, you could have all the things you think the lottery could bring you. *And* you'd be able to keep them, for they would be yours by right of consciousness. Affirming, declaring, deserving, and allowing are the steps to demonstrating riches far greater that you could ever win in a lottery.

Another thing that can keep you from prospering is being *dis-honest*. Whatever you give out comes back to you. Always. If you take from Life, then Life will take from you. It's that simple. You may feel that you don't steal, but are you counting the paper clips and stamps you're taking home from the office? Or are you a person who steals time or robs others of respect—or perhaps steals relationships? All these things count and are a way of saying to the Universe: "I don't really deserve the good in life. I have to sneak it and take it."

Become aware of the beliefs that may be blocking the flow of money in your life. Then change those beliefs and begin to create new, abundant thinking. Even if no one else in your family has done this, you can open your mind to the concept of money flowing into your life.

If you want to prosper, then you must use *prosperity thinking*. There are two prosperity affirmations that I've used for many years, and they work well for me. They'll also work for you. They are:

My income is constantly increasing,

and

I prosper wherever I turn.

♥

I had very little money when I started using these affirmations, but consistent practice has made them come true for me.

For a long time, I've believed that business is a place where we bless and prosper each other. I've never understood the concept of cutthroat business, where you try to cheat and put one over on the other person. That doesn't sound like a joyous way to live. There's so much abundance in this world—all we need to do is recognize that fact and share the wealth.

At Hay House, my publishing company, we've always been honest and honorable. We live up to our word, do our work well, and treat others with respect and generosity. When you live that way, it's impossible to keep the money away; the Universe rewards you at every possible turn. Today we have a fabulous reputation in the publishing world, and so much business that we're turning it away. We don't want to grow so big that we lose the personal touch.

If I, an abused child who didn't finish high school, can do it, *you can, too.* So once a day, stand with your arms open wide and say with joy:

"I am open and receptive to all the good and abundance in the Universe. Thank you, Life."

Life will hear you and respond.

POSITIVE
AFFIRMATIONS
FOR
PROSPERITY

I am a magnet for money.
Prosperity of every kind is
drawn to me.

· •●○ ·

I think big, and then I allow
myself to accept even more good
from Life.

· •●○ ·

Wherever it is that I work, I
am deeply appreciated and well
compensated.

· •●○ ·

Today is a delightful day.
Money comes to me in expected
and unexpected ways.

I have unlimited choices.
Opportunities are everywhere.

· · ● · ·

I truly believe that we are here to
bless and prosper each other.
I reflect this belief
in my daily interactions.

· · ● · ·

I support others in becoming
prosperous and in turn Life
supports me in wondrous ways.

· · ● · ·

I now do work I love,
and I am well paid for it.

· · ● · ·

The money that comes to me
today is a pleasure to handle.
I save some and spend some.

· · ● · ·

I live in a loving, abundant,
harmonious universe,
and I am grateful.

· · • · ·

I am now willing to be open
to the unlimited prosperity that
exists everywhere.

· · • · ·

Money is a state of mind that
supports me. I allow prosperity to
enter my life on a higher level
than ever before.

· · • · ·

I radiate success, and prosper
wherever I turn.

· · • · ·

Life supplies all my needs in great
abundance. I trust Life.

The Law of Attraction
brings only good into my life.

· •●○ ·

I move from poverty thinking
to prosperity thinking, and my
finances reflect this change.

· •●○ ·

I delight in the financial security
that is a constant in my life.

· •●○ ·

MORE
POSITIVE
AFFIRMATIONS
FOR
PROSPERITY

The more grateful I am for the
wealth and abundance in my
life, the more reasons I find
to be grateful.

⋅•●•⋅

I express gratitude for all the
good in my life. Each day brings
wonderful new surprises.

⋅•●•⋅

I pay my bills with love,
and I rejoice as I write out each check.
Abundance flows freely through me.

·∙●∘·

At this very moment, enormous
wealth and power are available to me.
I choose to feel worthy and deserving.

·∙●∘·

I deserve the best, and I accept
the best now.

·∙●∘·

I release all resistance to
money, and I now allow it to
flow joyously into my life.

· · ● ○ · ·

My good comes from
everywhere and everyone.

· · ● ○ · ·

CHAPTER 4

CREATIVITY

I do something new
or at least different
every day.

You can never express yourself creatively by talking or thinking about what a klutz you are. If you say, "I am not creative," then that's an affirmation that will be true for you for as long as you continue to use it. There's an innate creativity flowing through you, and if you let it out, it will surprise and delight you. You're tapped in to the creative flow of energy in the Universe. Some of you may express yourself more creatively than others, but everyone can do it.

We create our lives every day. Each of us has unique talents and abilities. Unfortunately, too many of us had well-meaning adults stifle that creativity when we were children. I had a teacher who once told me I couldn't dance because I was too tall. A friend was told he couldn't draw because he drew the wrong tree. It's all so silly. But we were obedient children and believed the messages. Now we can go beyond them.

Another false assumption is that you must be an artist to be creative. That's just one form of creativity, and there are so many more. You're creating every moment of your life—from the most common, ordinary creation of new cells in your body, to your emotional responses, to your present job, to your bank account, to your relationships with friends, and to your very attitudes about yourself. It's all creativity.

Also, you could be a really good bed maker, you could cook delicious food, you could do your job creatively, you could be an artist in the garden, or you could be inventive in the ways in which you're kind to others. These are a few of the millions of ways of expressing oneself creatively. No matter which way you choose, you'll want to feel satisfaction and be deeply fulfilled by all that you do.

You're divinely guided by Spirit at all times. Know that Spirit makes no mistakes. When there's a strong desire within you to express or create something, know that this feeling is Divine discontent. Your longing is your calling—and no matter what it is, if you go with it, you'll be guided, guarded, and assured of success. When a purpose or path is laid before you, you have the choice to just trust and let it flow, or remain stuck in fear. Trusting the perfection that resides within you is the key. I know that it can be frightening! Everybody is afraid of something, but you can do it anyway. Remember, the Universe loves you and wants you to succeed at everything you do.

You're expressing yourself creatively every moment of every day. You're being you in your own unique way. Knowing that, you can now release any false mental beliefs that you're not creative, and go forward with each and every project that comes to mind.

Never make the mistake of thinking that you're too old for anything. My own life didn't begin to have meaning until I was in my mid-40s, when I started teaching. At age 50, I started my publishing company on a very small scale. At 55, I ventured into the world of computers, taking classes and overcoming my fear of them. At 60, I started my first garden and have become an avid organic gardener who grows her own food. At 70, I enrolled in a children's art class. A few years later, I totally changed my handwriting—I became inspired by author Vimala Rodgers, who wrote *Your Handwriting*

Can Change Your Life. At 75, I graduated to an adult art class and have started to sell my paintings. My current art teacher wants me to get involved with sculpture next. And recently, I took up yoga, and my body is making positive changes.

A few months ago, I decided to stretch myself in areas that scared me, and I took up ballroom dancing. Now I'm taking several classes a week, and I'm fulfilling my childhood dream of learning to dance.

I love to learn things I haven't experienced. Who knows what I'll do in the future? What I do know is that I'll be doing my affirmations and expressing new creativity until the day I leave this planet.

If there's a particular project you want to work on, or if you just want to be more creative in general, then you can use some of the following affirmations. Use them joyously as you release your creativity in a million and one different projects.

POSITIVE
AFFIRMATIONS
FOR
CREATIVITY

I release all resistance to
expressing my creativity fully.

· ·●· ·

I am always in touch with my
creative source.

· ·●· ·

I create easily and effortlessly
when I let my thoughts come from
the loving space of my own heart.

· ·●· ·

I do something new or at least
different—every day.

There is ample time
and opportunity for
creative expression in
whatever area I choose.

· • ● ∘ ·

My family totally supports me in
fulfilling my dreams.

· • ● ∘ ·

All of my creative projects bring
me great satisfaction.

· • ● ∘ ·

I know that I can create
miracles in my life.

· • ● ∘ ·

I feel good expressing myself in
all sorts of creative ways.

· • ● ∘ ·

I am my own unique self: special,
creative, and wonderful.

' ・●○ ・

I direct my creative talents
toward music, art, dance, writing—
anything that gives me pleasure.

' ・●○ ・

The key to creativity is knowing
that my thinking creates my
experience. I use this key in
every area of my life.

' ・●○ ・

I am a clear thinker, and I express
myself with ease.

' ・●○ ・

I am learning to be more
creative every day.

I am discovering talents
I did not know I had.

· •●° ·

My job allows me to express my
talents and abilities, and I rejoice
in this employment.

· •●° ·

My potential is unlimited.

· •●° ·

My innate creativity surprises
and delights me.

· •●° ·

I am safe, and I am fulfilled
in all that I do.

· •●° ·

My talents are in demand, and my
unique gifts are appreciated by
those around me.

MORE
POSITIVE
AFFIRMATIONS
FOR
CREATIVITY

Life is never stuck, stagnant,
or stale, for each moment is
ever-new and fresh.

· ·●◦ ·

My heart is the center of my
power. I follow my heart.

· ·●◦ ·

I am a joyous, creative
expression of Life.

· ·●◦ ·

Ideas comes to me easily
and effortlessly.

CHAPTER 5

RELATIONSHIPS/ ROMANCE

I have a wonderful lover,
and we are both happy
and at peace.

Personal relationships always seem to be the first priority for so many of us. Unfortunately, hunting for love doesn't always attract the right partner because our reasons for wanting love may be unclear. We think, *Oh, if I only had someone who loved me, my life would be so much better.* That's not the way it works.

There's a big difference between the *need* for love and being *needy* for love. When you're needy for love, it means that you're missing love and approval from the most important person you know—yourself. You may become involved in relationships that are codependent and ineffectual for both partners.

You can never create love in your life by talking or thinking about being lonely. Feeling lonely and needy just pushes people away. Nor can you heal a relationship in your life by talking or thinking about how awful it is. This only places attention on what's wrong. You want to turn your thoughts away from the problem and create new thoughts that will produce a *solution.* Arguing for your limitations is just resistance, and resistance is simply a delay tactic. It's another way of saying, "I'm not good enough to have what I'm asking for."

The first relationship to improve is the one you have with yourself. When you're happy with yourself, then all of your other relationships improve, too. A happy person is very attractive to others. If you're looking for more love, then you need to love yourself more. This means no criticism, no complaining, no blaming, no whining, and no choosing to feel lonely. It means being very content with yourself in the present moment and choosing to think thoughts that make you feel good now.

♥

There's no one way to experience love, for we all experience love in different ways. For some of us to really experience love, we need to *feel* love, through being hugged and touched. Some of us, however, need to *hear* the words *"I love you."* Others need to *see* a demonstration of love, like a gift of flowers. Our preferred way of experiencing love is often the way we feel most comfortable demonstrating it back.

I suggest that you work on loving yourself nonstop. Demonstrate the growing love you have for yourself. Treat yourself to romance and love. Show yourself how special you are. Pamper yourself. Buy yourself flowers for your home; and surround yourself with colors, textures, and scents that please you. Life always mirrors back to us the feelings we have inside. As you develop your inner sense of love and romance, the right person to share your growing sense of intimacy with will be attracted to you like a magnet.

If you want to go from loneliness thinking to fulfillment thinking, then you need to think in terms of creating a loving mental atmosphere within you and around you. Do let all those negative thoughts about love and romance just fade away; and instead, think about sharing love, approval, and acceptance with everyone you meet.

When you're able to contribute to the fulfillment of your own needs, then you won't be so needy and codependent. It has to do with how much you love yourself. When you truly love who you are, you stay centered, calm, and secure, and your relationships at home as well as at work are wonderful. You'll find yourself reacting to various situations and people differently. Matters that once may have been desperately important won't seem quite as crucial anymore. New people will enter your life, and perhaps some old ones will disappear—this can be kind of scary at first—but it can also be wonderful, refreshing, and exciting.

♥

Once you're clear about this issue in your mind, and you know what you want in a relationship, you must go out and be with people. No one is going to suddenly appear at your doorstep. A good way to meet people is in a support group or night class. These types of get-togethers enable you to connect with people who are like-minded or who are involved in the same pursuits. It's amazing how quickly you can meet new friends. Be open and receptive, and the Universe will respond to you, bringing you your highest good.

Remember, when you think joyous thoughts, you'll be a happy person, everyone will want to be with you, and all of your current relationships will improve.

POSITIVE
AFFIRMATIONS
FOR
ATTRACTING
LOVE & ROMANCE

From time to time, I ask those
I love, "How can I love you more?"

· · ● ○ · ·

I choose to see clearly with eyes of
love. I love what I see.

· · ● ○ · ·

Love happens! I release the
desperate need for love, and
instead, allow it to find me in the
perfect time-space sequence.

· · ● ○ · ·

Love is around every corner,
and joy fills my entire world.

I have come to this planet to learn
to love myself more, and to share
that love with all those around me.

' • ● ° •

My partner is the love of my life.
We adore each other.

' • ● ° •

Life is very simple. What I give
out comes back to me. Today
I choose to give love.

' • ● ° •

I rejoice in the love
I encounter every day.

' • ● ° •

I am comfortable looking in the
mirror, saying "I love you,
I really love you."

' • ● ° •

I now deserve love, romance, and joy—and all the good that Life has to offer me.

· • ● • ·

Love is powerful—your love and my love. Love brings us peace on Earth.

· • ● • ·

Love is all there is!

· • ● • ·

I am surrounded by love. All is well.

· • ● • ·

I draw love and romance into my life, and I accept it now.

· • ● • ·

My heart is open. I speak with loving words.

I have a wonderful lover, and we
are both happy and at peace.

· ·●o ·

Deep at the center of my being is
an Infinite Well of Love.

· ·●o ·

I am in a joyous, intimate
relationship with a person who
truly loves me.

MORE
POSITIVE
AFFIRMATIONS
FOR
ATTRACTING
LOVE & ROMANCE

I come from the loving space
of my heart, and I know that
love opens all doors.

I am beautiful, and everybody
loves me. I am greeted by love
wherever I go.

· •●○ ·

I am safe in all my relationships,
and I give and receive lots of love.

· •●○ ·

I attract only healthy
relationships.
I am always treated well.

· •●○ ·

I am very thankful for
all the love in my life.
I find it everywhere.

· •●○ ·

Long-lasting, loving
relationships brighten my life.

· •●○ ·

CHAPTER 6

JOB SUCCESS

Limitations are merely
opportunities to grow.
I use them as stepping-stones
to success.

♥

55

Finding success in a career is a major problem for many people. However, you can always have a successful job if you simply change the way you think about work. You'll never find work a pleasure if you hate your job or you can't stand your boss. What a terrible affirmation that is. It will be impossible for you to ever attract a great job with that belief system. If you want to enjoy your time at work, then you must change your thinking. I'm a great believer in blessing every person, place, and thing in the workplace with love. Begin with your current job: Affirm that it is merely a stepping-stone to far greater positions.

You're in your current job because of things you believed in the past. You drew it to you by your thinking. Perhaps you learned your attitude toward work from your parents. No matter—you can change your thinking now. So bless with love your boss, your co-workers, the location, the building, the elevators or stairs, the offices, the furniture, and each and every customer. This creates a loving mental atmosphere within you, and the entire environment will respond to it.

I've never understood the reasoning behind belittling or berating others at work. If you're an owner, a manager, or a supervisor, how can you possibly expect to get the best work from others if they're frightened or resentful? We all want to be appreciated, acknowledged, and encouraged. If you support your employees and give them respect, then they'll give you the best work they can.

Please don't believe that it's hard to get a job. That may be true for many, but it doesn't have to be true for you. You only need one job, and your consciousness will then open the pathway for you. Don't have faith in fear. When you hear of negative trends in business or in the economy, immediately affirm: *"It may be true for some, but it is not true for me. I always prosper no matter where I am or what is going on."*

People often ask me for affirmations to make their relationships at work smoother. In fact, for many people this is a really big issue in their lives. I'm deeply aware that whatever I give out comes back to me multiplied. This is true everywhere, including at work. In the workplace, it's important to know that every employee (and employer) has been attracted by the action of love, for it's his or her Divine right place here at this very moment. Divine harmony permeates us all, and we can flow together in the workplace in a most productive and joyous way.

There aren't any problems that don't have solutions. There aren't any questions without answers. Choose to go beyond the problem to seek the Divine solution to any type of discord that seems to appear. Be willing to learn from any strife or confusion as it comes up. It's important to release all blame, and turn within to seek the truth. And be willing to release whatever pattern may be in your consciousness that has contributed to the situation.

You know that you're successful in all that you do. You're inspired and productive. You serve others willingly and gladly. Divine harmony reigns supreme within and around you and within and around each and every person in your workplace.

If you like your job but feel that you're not getting paid enough, then bless your current salary with love. Expressing gratitude for what you have now enables your income to grow. And please, absolutely no more complaining about the job or your co-workers. Your consciousness put you where you are now. Your changing consciousness can lift you to a better position. You can do it!

During your workday, there are a number of things you can do to release tension. Here are a few of my suggestions:

- Before you go to work every day, do this simple exercise: Just sit comfortably and concentrate on your breath. Whenever you notice thoughts coming in, gently bring your awareness back to your breath. Give yourself at least 10 or 15 minutes to dwell in the silence each day. There's nothing difficult or tricky to this.

- Write or type this affirmation and put it where you can see it at work every day:

My job is a peaceful haven.
I bless my job with love.

I put love in every corner, and my job lovingly responds with warmth and comfort. I am at peace.

When you start to think about your boss, say this affirmation to yourself:

> ## I only give out that which
> ## I wish to receive.
>
> ## My love and acceptance of others
> ## is mirrored to me in every way.

Refuse to be limited in any way by human-mind thinking. Your life can be filled with love and joy because your work is a Divine idea. Remember to say to yourself every day before going to work:

> ## No matter where I am, there is only
> ## infinite good, infinite wisdom, infinite
> ## harmony, and infinite love.

POSITIVE
AFFIRMATIONS
FOR
JOB SUCCESS

My joy allows me to express my
talents and abilities, and I am
grateful for this employment.

· • ● • ·

The joy I find in my career is
reflected in my overall happiness.

· • ● • ·

Making decisions is easy for me.
I welcome new ideas, and I follow
through with what I say.

· • ● • ·

At my job, my co-workers
and I encourage each other's
growth and success.

When I wake up in the morning,
I plan for a good day. My
anticipation attracts positive
experiences to me.

· · ● ° ·

The perfect job is looking for
me, and we are being brought
together now.

· · ● ° ·

I truly believe that we are here
to bless and prosper each other.
I reflect this belief in my
daily interactions.

· · ● ° ·

I choose healthy stimulation.
During breaks at work, I speak
positively with others and listen
with compassion.

· · ● ° ·

I am at ease speaking in
front other others. I have
confidence in myself.

· · ● ○ ·

When I encounter problems on the
job, I am willing to ask for help.

· · ● ○ ·

I create a good feeling at work.
I realize that there are laws
that govern the Universe, and
I work with these laws in
every area of my life.

· · ● ○ ·

I know that when I do my
best at my job, I am rewarded
in all sorts of ways.

· · ● ○ ·

When it is time for a new job,
the perfect position will
present itself easily.

· ·●· ·

Limitations are merely
opportunities to grow. I use them
as stepping-stones to success.

· ·●· ·

Opportunities are everywhere.
I have a multitude of choices.

· ·●· ·

I am the star in my own movie.
I am also the writer and the
director. I create wonderful
roles for myself in my work
environment.

· ·●· ·

MORE
POSITIVE
AFFIRMATIONS
FOR
JOB SUCCESS

I handle authority with ease, and
I am always respected in return.

· • ● ○ ·

Working together is part of
the purpose of life. I love the
people I work with.

· • ● ○ ·

I deserve to have a successful
career, and I accept it now.

· • ● ○ ·

Everyone I encounter at
work today has my best
interests at heart.

My job supports the unfoldment of my highest potential. I am successful at everything I do.

· · ● ○ ·

I am very good at giving encouragement and positive feedback to others.

· · ● ○ ·

I have unlimited potential. Only good lies before me.

· · ● ○ ·

My workplace is a pleasure to be in. There is mutual respect among my co-workers.

· · ● ○ ·

CHAPTER 7

STRESS-FREE LIVING

I have the strength
to remain calm in the
face of change.

This is the moment in which you're either enjoying or not enjoying your life. What you're thinking is creating the way you feel in your body right now, and it's also creating your experiences of tomorrow. If you're stressing out over every little thing and making mountains out of molehills, you'll never find inner peace.

We talk a lot about stress these days. Everyone seems to be stressed out by something. *Stress* seems to be a buzzword, and we use it to the point where I think it's a cop-out: "I'm so stressed," or "This is so stressful," or "All this stress, stress, stress."

I think that stress is a fearful reaction to life's constant changes. It's an excuse we often use for not taking responsibility for our feelings. If we can put the blame out there on someone or something, then we can just play the innocent victim. Being the victim doesn't make us feel good, and it doesn't change the situation.

Often we're stressing ourselves out because we have our priorities mixed up. So many of us feel that money is the most important thing in our lives. This is simply not true. There's something far more important and precious to us—without which we couldn't live. What is that? It's our *breath*.

Our breath is the most precious substance in our lives, and yet we totally take it for granted that when we exhale, our next breath will be there. If we didn't take another breath, we wouldn't last three minutes. Now if the Power that created us has given us enough breath to last as long as we shall live, can't we have faith that everything else we need will also be supplied?

When we trust Life to take care of all our little problems, then stress just melts away.

You don't have time to waste on negative thinking or emotions, because that only creates more of what you say you don't want. If you're doing some positive affirmations and you're not getting the results you desire, then check to see how often during the day you allow yourself to feel bad or upset. These emotions are probably just the thing that's frustrating you, delaying the manifestation of your affirmations, and stopping the flow of your good.

The next time you realize how stressed you are, ask yourself what's scaring you. Stress is just fear, it's that simple. You don't need to be afraid of life or your own emotions. Find out what you're doing to yourself that's creating this fear within you. Your inner goal is joy, harmony, and peace. Harmony is being at peace with yourself. It's not possible to have stress and inner harmony at the same time. When you're at peace, you do one thing at a time. You don't let things get to you.

So when you feel stressed, do something to release the fear: breathe deeply or go for a brisk walk. Affirm to yourself:

I am the only power in my world; and I create a peaceful, loving, joyful, fulfilling life.

You want to move through life feeling safe. Don't give a little word like *stress* a lot of power. Don't use it as an excuse for creating tension in your body. Nothing—no person, place, or thing—has any power over you. You're the only thinker in your mind, and your thoughts are the ones that create your life.

So train yourself to think thoughts that make you feel good. That way you'll always be creating your life *out of* joy and *in* joy. Joy always brings more to be joyous about.

♥
69

POSITIVE
AFFIRMATIONS
FOR
STRESS-FREE LIVING

I let go of all fear and doubt,
and life becomes simple
and easy for me.

·˙•○·˙

I create a stress-free world
for myself.

·˙•○·˙

I relax all of my neck muscles,
and I let go of any tension in my
shoulders.

·˙•○·˙

I slowly breathe in and out, and
I find myself relaxing more and
more with each breath.

I am a capable person, and
I can handle anything that
comes my way.

· •●• ·

I am centered and focused.
I feel more secure each day.

· •●• ·

I am even-tempered and
emotionally well balanced.

· •●• ·

I am at ease with myself, and I am
at ease with other people.

· •●• ·

I am safe when I express my
feelings. I can be serene in any
situation.

· •●• ·

I have a wonderful relationship
with my friends, family members,
and co-workers. I am appreciated.

· · ● ○ ·

I am comfortable with my
finances. I am always able to pay
my bills on time.

· · ● ○ ·

Financial security puts me at ease
and makes me feel good about
my future.

· · ● ○ ·

I am always in a loving
atmosphere—both
at home and at work.

· · ● ○ ·

I trust myself to deal with
any problems that arise
during the day.

· · ● · ·

I realize that stress is only fear.
I now release all fears.

· · ● · ·

I let go of childhood fears.
I am a secure, empowered
human being.

· · ● · ·

When I feel tense, I remember
to relax all of the muscles
and organs of my body.

· · ● · ·

I let go of all negativity that rests
in my body and mind.

· · ● · ·

MORE
POSITIVE
AFFIRMATIONS
FOR
STRESS-FREE LIVING

I am in the process of
making positive changes in
all areas of my life.

* • ° *

I have the strength to remain
calm in the face of change.

* • ° *

I am willing to learn. The more
I learn, the more I grow.

* • ° *

No matter how old I am, I can always learn more, and I do so with confidence.

· •●◦ ·

I meditate on a regular basis and reap benefits from this practice.

· •●◦ ·

I close my eyes, think positive thoughts, and breathe goodness in and out.

· •●◦ ·

CHAPTER 8

SELF-ESTEEM

I move through life and
know that I am safe—
Divinely protected
and guided.

You'll never have good self-esteem if you have negative thoughts about yourself.

Self-esteem is merely feeling good about yourself, and when you do so, you develop confidence. Confidence then builds self-esteem—each step feeds upon the other. Once you get the rhythm going, you can accomplish almost anything.

Since self-esteem is what you think about yourself, you have the freedom to think anything you want. So why would you want to belittle yourself?

You were born extremely confident. You came into this world knowing how wonderful you are. You were so perfect when you were a tiny baby. You didn't have to do anything—you were already perfect—and you acted as if you were aware of that. You knew you were the center of the Universe. You weren't afraid to ask for what you wanted. You freely expressed your emotions. Your mother knew when you were angry; in fact, the entire neighborhood knew it. And when you were happy, your smile lit up the whole room. You were so full of love and confidence.

Little babies will die if they don't get love. Once we're older, we learn to live without love, but no baby will stand for that. Babies also love every inch of their bodies, even their own feces. They have no guilt, no shame, no comparisons. They know they're unique and wonderful.

You were like that. Then somewhere during your childhood, your well-meaning parents passed on their own insecure feelings and taught you feelings of inadequacy and fear. At that point, you began to deny your own magnificence. These thoughts and feelings were never true, and they certainly aren't true now. So I want to bring you back to the time when you really knew how to love yourself by talking about mirror work.

Mirror work is simple and very powerful. It simply involves looking into a mirror when you say your affirmations. Mirrors reflect our true feelings back to us. As children, we received most of our negative messages from adults, many of them looking us straight in the eye and perhaps even shaking a finger at us. Today, when most of us look into a mirror, we'll say something negative. We either criticize our looks, or berate ourselves for something else.

To look yourself in the eye and make a positive declaration is one of the quickest ways to get positive results with affirmations. I ask people to look in their eyes and say something positive about themselves every time they pass a mirror.

If something unpleasant happens to you during the day, immediately go to the mirror and say: *"I love you anyway."* Events come and go, but the love you have for yourself can be constant, and it's the most important quality you possess in life. If something wonderful happens, go to the mirror and say, *"Thank you."* Acknowledge yourself for creating this wonderful experience.

First thing in the morning and last thing in the evening, I want you to look into your eyes and say: *"I love you, I really love you. And I accept you exactly as you are."* It can be tough at first, but if you stick with it, in a short time this affirmation will be true for you. Won't that be fun!

You'll find that as your self-love grows, so will your self-respect, and any changes that you find yourself needing to make will be easier to accomplish when you know that they're the right ones for you. Love is never outside yourself—it's always within you. As you're more loving, you'll be more lovable.

So choose new thoughts to *think* about yourself, and choose new words to *tell* yourself how magnificent you are and that you deserve all the good that Life has to offer.

POSITIVE
AFFIRMATIONS
FOR
SELF-ESTEEM

I am totally adequate
for all situations.

· ·●· ·

I choose to feel good about myself.
I am worthy of my own love.

· ·●· ·

I stand on my own two feet.
I accept and use my own power.

· ·●· ·

It is safe for me to speak up
for myself.

· ·●· ·

It does not matter what other
people say or do. What matters is
how I choose to react and what
I choose to believe about myself.

' • ● ○ •

I take a deep breath and
allow myself to relax.
My entire body calms down.

' • ● ○ •

I am loved and accepted exactly as
I am, right here and right now.

' • ● ○ •

I see the world through eyes
of love and acceptance.
All is well in my world.

' • ● ○ •

My self-esteem is high because
I honor who I am.

' • ● ○ •

I willingly release any need for
struggle or suffering.
I deserve all that is good.

· ·●° ·

My life gets more fabulous every
day. I look forward to what each
new hour brings.

· ·●° ·

I am neither too little nor too
much, and I do not have to prove
myself to anyone.

· ·●° ·

I am a radiant being,
enjoying life to the fullest.

· ·●° ·

Today, no person, place, or thing
can irritate or annoy me.
I choose to be at peace.

· ·●° ·

For every problem that I may create, I am confident that I can find a solution.

· ·●· ·

Life supports me in every possible way.

· ·●· ·

My consciousness is filled with healthy, positive, loving thoughts that reflect themselves in my experience.

· ·●· ·

I move through life and know that I am safe—Divinely protected and guided.

· ·●· ·

MORE
POSITIVE
AFFIRMATIONS
FOR
SELF-ESTEEM

I accept others as they are;
and they, in turn, accept me.

• • ● • •

I am wonderful, and I feel great.
I am grateful for my life.

• • ● • •

This is the only time I get to live
today. I choose to enjoy it.

• • ● • •

I have the self-esteem, power, and
confidence to move forward in life
with ease.

· •●○ ·

The greatest gift I can give myself
is unconditional love.

· •●○ ·

I love myself exactly as I am.
I no longer wait to be perfect in
order to love myself.

· •●○ ·

IN CONCLUSION

Once you've done your affirmations, then it's time to release them and let them go. You've decided what you want. You've affirmed them in both thought and word. Now you must release them to the Universe so that the laws of Life can bring them to you.

If you worry and fret about *how* your affirmations will come true, you're just delaying the whole process. It's *not* your job to figure out how to bring your affirmations to fruition. The way the Laws of Attraction work, you declare that you have something, and then the Universe brings it to you. The Universe is far more clever than you are and knows every possible way to make your affirmations come true. The only reason for delay and for seemingly denying you is that there's a part of you *that doesn't believe that you deserve it*. Or perhaps your beliefs are so strong that they overpower your affirmations.

If you're declaring: *"My income is increasing,"* and it isn't, then perhaps you have old, deep-seated beliefs that you don't deserve

♥

to prosper. Or maybe your family had strong negative beliefs about money, and there's a part of you that still accepts those beliefs.

As little children, we're so obedient that we're willing to accept our parents' beliefs about life and continue to operate under them for the rest of our lives . . . until we choose to really look at those beliefs and examine them.

Your mother or father may have constantly said, "Oh, money is hard to come by." Now without even knowing it, you still have that belief in your own consciousness. If you believe that, then the Universe can't bring you more income until you release that thought.

I often ask people to look at what their family's beliefs were about various subjects. If prosperity is your issue, then take out a large sheet of paper and write down all the things your family said about money when you were a child. If you find any negative statements (remember these were *all* affirmations for your family members), then your job is to turn those negative beliefs into positive affirmations. Free yourself from the tyranny of your parents' negative affirmations, and you'll open yourself to the abundant flow of good in every area of your life.

Please don't be discouraged by any setbacks. You're learning a new process. As you become proficient at it, your life will become easier and easier.

Remember . . .

No matter how wonderful
the present moment is, the future
can be even more fulfilling and joyous.

The Universe always waits in smiling
repose for us to align our thinking
with its laws. When we are in
alignment, everything flows.

It is possible. You can do it.
I can do it. We *all* can do it.

Make the effort. You will be so pleased.
Your whole world will change for the better.

ABOUT THE AUTHOR

Louise Hay was an inspirational teacher who educated millions since the 1984 publication of her bestseller *You Can Heal Your Life*, which has more than 50 million copies in print worldwide. Renowned for demonstrating the power of affirmations to bring about positive change, Louise was the author of more than 30 books for adults and children, including the bestsellers *The Power Is Within You* and *Heal Your Body*. In addition to her books, Louise produced numerous audio and video programs, card decks, online courses, and other resources for leading a healthy, joyous, and fulfilling life.

WEBSITES:
www.louisehay.com
www.healyourlife.com
www.facebook.com/louiselhay

HAY HOUSE TITLES OF
RELATED INTEREST

YOU CAN HEAL YOUR LIFE,
the movie, starring Louise Hay & Friends
*(available as a 1-DVD program, an expanded 2-DVD set,
and an online streaming video)*

Learn more at www.hayhouse.com/louise-movie

THE SHIFT,
the movie,
starring Dr. Wayne W. Dyer
*(available as a 1-DVD program, an expanded 2-DVD set,
and an online streaming video)*

Learn more at www.hayhouse.com/the-shift-movie

*Black Girl In Love (with Herself):
A Guide to Self-Love, Healing,
and Creating the Life You Truly Deserve*
by Trey Anthony

Get Over It!: Thought Therapy for Healing the Hard Stuff
by Iyanla Vanzant

*How to Love Yourself (and Sometimes Other People):
Spiritual Advice for Modern Relationships*
by Meggan Watterson and Lodro Rinzler

*Super Attractor: Methods for Manifesting a
Life beyond Your Wildest Dreams*
by Gabrielle Bernstein

**All of the above are available at your local bookstore,
or may be ordered by contacting Hay House (see next page).**

We hope you enjoyed this Hay House book. If you'd like to receive our online catalog featuring additional information on Hay House books and products, or if you'd like to find out more about the Hay Foundation, please contact:

Hay House, Inc., P.O. Box 5100, Carlsbad, CA 92018-5100
(760) 431-7695 or (800) 654-5126
(760) 431-6948 (fax) or (800) 650-5115 (fax)
www.hayhouse.com® • www.hayfoundation.org

———

Published in Australia by: Hay House Australia Pty. Ltd.,
18/36 Ralph St., Alexandria NSW 2015
Phone: 612-9669-4299 • *Fax:* 612-9669-4144
www.hayhouse.com.au

Published in the United Kingdom by: Hay House UK, Ltd.,
The Sixth Floor, Watson House, 54 Baker Street, London W1U 7BU
Phone: +44 (0)20 3927 7290 • *Fax:* +44 (0)20 3927 7291
www.hayhouse.co.uk

Published in India by: Hay House Publishers India,
Muskaan Complex, Plot No. 3, B-2, Vasant Kunj, New Delhi 110 070
Phone: 91-11-4176-1620 • *Fax:* 91-11-4176-1630
www.hayhouse.co.in

———

Access New Knowledge.
Anytime. Anywhere.

Learn and evolve at your own pace
with the world's leading experts.

www.hayhouseU.com